Religions and Beliefs

Series Editor: Ina Taylor

Sikhism

Manjit Kaur
Dilwyn Hunt

Nelson Thornes

Published in 2007 by:
Nelson Thornes Ltd
Delta Place
27 Bath Road
CHELTENHAM
GL53 7TH
United Kingdom

09 10 11 / 10 9 8 7 6 5 4 3

A catalogue record for this book is available from the British Library

ISBN 978 0 7487 9675 5

Edited by Judi Hunter
Picture research by Sue Sharp
Illustrations by Angela Lumley and Harry Venning
Page make-up by eMC Design Ltd

Printed and bound in China by 1010 Printing International Ltd.

Acknowledgements

With thanks to the following for permission to reproduce photographs and other copyright material in this book:

Cover photo: David Davis Photoproductions/Alamy

Alamy/World Religions Photo Library: 26; Andes Press Agency/Carlos Reyes Manzo: 12, 34, 42; Ark Religion/Alamy: 14, 36; Art Directors and Trip: 13; Barbara Penoyar/Photodisc 16 (NT): 46; Circa Religion Photo Library/John Smith: 57; Corbis/Charles & Josette Lenars: 30B; Corbis/Eleanor Bentall: 21; Corbis/Kazuyoshi Nomachi: 50; Corbis/Richard T. Nowitz: 62; Corel 337 (NT): 8; Dr Harinder Singh Bedi: 23B; Greenhill/Alamy: 11; Groundwork Greater Nottingham: 55; Ina Taylor: 45; International Rice Research Institute: 23C; Janine Wiedel Photolibrary/Alamy: 39; Jeff Morgan/Alamy: 59B; John Cole/Alamy: 7B, 35; Khalsa Aid/Ravinder Singh: 48, 49; Martin Sookias/Nelson Thornes (NT): 27; Nabil Mounzer/epa/Corbis: 61; Neil Cooper/Alamy: 54; Photodisc 10 (NT): 6; Rex Features/Eddie Mulholland: 43; Sally & Richard Greenhill: 30A; Science Photo Library/Jim Varney: 25; Stan Kujawa/Alamy: 60; Trip/Alamy: 5, 59A; Visual Arts Library/Alamy: 22; World Religions/Alamy: 17, 19

The Khalsa Wood project (page 55) was organised by Nottingham Council in association with Groundwork Greater Nottingham, the Sikh Youth and Community Service, Bestwood Country Park, with funding from the National Lottery and support from the Sikh community.

Every effort has been made to contact copyright holders. The publishers apologise to anyone whose rights have been inadvertently overlooked, and will be happy to rectify any errors or omissions.

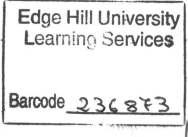

Contents

 # Fast facts about Sikhism

Q What is Sikhism?

Sikhism is the name of the religion followed by Sikhs. The word 'Sikh' comes from Punjabi and means 'someone who learns'. Sikhs are people who believe in one God and follow the teachings of the Ten Gurus of Sikhism. The word 'Guru' means 'teacher' and Sikhs believe that the Ten Gurus were special people who passed on God's teachings.

Q Are there different types of Sikhs?

As with all religions, there are Sikhs who practise their religion in slightly different ways.

Q When did it begin?

Sikhism is the youngest of the six major world religions. It began in the Punjab area of India in the fifteenth century.

Q How many Sikhs are there in the world today?

There are around 20 million Sikhs in the world today. Most of these live in India but there are around half a million Sikhs living in Britain, which makes it the UK's fourth largest religion.

Looking for meaning

A This painting shows the first great teacher of Sikhism, Guru Nanak (1469–1539).

For some 500 years, Sikhism has proved itself to be a faith which inspires people's lives. It has enabled people to live lives of joyful friendliness, inner peace and often of great courage.

- What lies behind this religion?

- How does Sikhism try to make sense of life?

- What values can be learned from Sikhism?

Beliefs about God

objective

to learn what Sikhs believe about God

glossary

Il Onkar
Langar
Mool Mantra
Sikh

All around us there are things which, most of the time, our senses have no direct knowledge of. Gravity, radio waves and electricity have no shape or form. They cannot be seen and yet none of us are in any doubt that such things exist.

For every **Sikh** there is yet another invisible, eternal presence. This presence has no shape or form. This presence is what brought about the universe in the first place. Whether you believe or do not believe in this presence, Sikhs believe it is fundamental to everyone's life. This presence is what most people call 'God'.

For Sikhs, there is only one God. Sikh beliefs are encompassed in the **Mool Mantra**. It begins with **Il Onkar** meaning, 'There is one God'. God is the creator of the universe and of everything in it. God exists outside of time. In Sikhism it is nonsense to say that God is very old as if God is ageing, just as it is nonsense to say gravity is ageing. God has no gender. God isn't male or female.

Sikhs do not believe that God has ever taken the shape of a human or animal. God has not taken a physical form.

However, vital to Sikhs is the belief that God is personal. God isn't like gravity, radio waves or electricity. Gravity, radio waves and electricity don't make choices. Nobody has a relationship with gravity. We don't wake up in the morning and say, 'Thank you gravity for keeping my feet on the planet!' To Sikhs, God isn't an abstract, emotionless force.

A What happens when a ball is thrown into the air? What happens when a radio is turned on? Does the radio conjure up the radio waves? The radio waves are always there and yet, somehow, they remain unseen.

Instead, for Sikhs, God is a being with whom we humans can have a relationship. In God, Sikhs are aware of an awesome beauty and power. God is described by Sikhs as being 'eternal truth'. The most fundamental truth about the universe is found in God. So God is the basis of knowing right from wrong. God is a moral being.

1 What *two* reasons might a person give for believing in God today?

2 Apart from Sikhism, name *two* other religions which believe in one God.

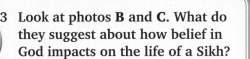

B Sikhs working in a **langar**.

3 Look at photos **B** and **C**. What do they suggest about how belief in God impacts on the life of a Sikh?

4 Design a poster which shows how Sikhism and *one* other religion are similar, but in some ways different, in their belief about God.

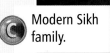

C Modern Sikh family.

God is also described as being 'fearless and without hatred'. God doesn't play tricks on humans. God isn't cruel. God doesn't punish people. A person in the presence of God would not know fear. Instead, they would know God's true majesty and be filled with awe and wonder. Therefore, a Sikh does not live in fear of God, quite the opposite. For Sikhs, God is to be loved, adored and, of course, worshipped.

5 Place the *six* statements below into a lucky dip hat. Without looking, pick out a statement. With a partner, explain what you think the statement means to the rest of the class.

● God is a moral being.
● God isn't cruel.
● God isn't a physical being.
● God is personal.
● God is beyond birth and death.
● God lives in everything.

7

Life's goal

objective

to learn what Sikhs believe about achieving life's goal

glossary

Gurdwara
Reincarnation
Sewa

Imagine running a cross-country marathon. Over many miles you've slogged through mud, tripped over branches, lost your footing in many pot-holes and have been soaked by rain. But now, at the top of a steep hill, you can see the finishing line. You are one of the lucky ones.

Sikhs believe that every human is, in a sense, at the end of a long marathon and the finish line is in sight. This is because Sikhs believe that we have passed through many lives. We have been born and have died many times. The belief that we have lived many lives is called **reincarnation**.

Of all the different types of life only humans can escape reincarnation. If you were born as a fish or a deer, you would not be able to escape. Only humans can break free and achieve the great goal. That goal, the final finishing line for all life, is union with God.

Sikhs believe that people will not achieve union with God simply by doing religious things such as performing rituals, making sacrifices or going to a temple, a **gurdwara**, or a church. Sikhism even teaches that doing what so-called highly religious people do will not work. For example, a holy person might fast, live a life of poverty, dress very simply and spend long hours in prayer or meditation. And yet none of this will guarantee union with God.

Sikhs believe that you cannot gain union with God by being a solitary person living life cut off from others. The real challenge is to be a holy person living in the world with everyone else.

Only by facing up to the challenge of living in the world can a person battle their way up the final steep hill of human life and so achieve union with God.

Sikhs believe that they should try to live life as a holy person while living in the real world. This involves being honest, fair, kind, hard working and generous. The challenge is doing this in spite of the corruption and dishonesty which may go on around you. An important part of this is to help and be of service to other people. This is called **Sewa**.

 Share and share alike.

Activity

1 Look at picture **B**. What questions for discussion does this picture raise for you?

2 Do others influence what you do? Is this a good thing? Give an example to make your point clear.

3 Is the Sikh claim that there is a final goal to life appealing to you? Explain your answer.

Humans and planet earth

Sikhs believe that God created the universe and everything in it. They also believe that every soul is a small part of God. Therefore, Sikhs value all life on the planet, but they believe that humans are closest to God as they are the only beings who can gain union with God. This does not mean that Sikhs think they can rule over all other living things, but it does mean that Sikhs believe they have a responsibility to look after God's creation.

Activity

4 Write a list of the similarities and differences between Sikh and Christian beliefs about the role of humans on the planet.

Is death the end?

No point avoiding the issue – everyone dies sooner or later. But what happens when we die? Is death simply the end? Do we just cease to exist? The great twentieth-century biologist and **atheist** J.B.S. Haldane certainly thought so. He said, 'When a man has died he is dead.'

The beginning, not the end

Sikhism, however, offers a very different vision of the future. Although Sikhs accept that our physical body will eventually just decompose, Sikhism teaches that all living things have a soul. The soul is not a material thing. It cannot decompose or rot. The soul cannot die. The soul is the inner presence of God and so, like God, it is immortal.

'The body is mere earth... but the soul that sees behind does not die.'

(Guru Nanak 1469–1539)

'He shall wander from womb to womb in the cycle of birth... So long as man is in love with the illusory goods of the world.'

(Guru Arjan 1563–1606)

Sikhism teaches that our soul will continuously be reborn in new physical bodies as long as we remain spiteful, selfish and besotted by trivial pleasures and worldly goals. World desires trap us in a constant cycle of reincarnation.

objective

to consider what Sikhs believe about life after death

glossary

Atheist
Guru Arjan

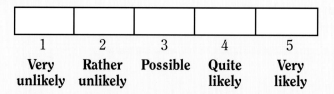

1 a Do you believe that every one of us has lived many lives before? Using the scale 1–5 below, decide how likely this is.

1	2	3	4	5
Very unlikely	Rather unlikely	Possible	Quite likely	Very likely

b Write the number representing your view on a piece of paper. Fold and place the class' papers into a box and shake them up. Ask everyone to take one of the papers. Everyone with number 1 then forms a line. Do the same for numbers 2, 3, 4 and 5 until the class has formed a human bar chart.

c In groups, suggest good reasons why some people believe that reincarnation is very likely and why others think it is very unlikely.

A Sikh funeral.

Sikhs believe that death is a time for praising God and remembering the person who has died. It is not a time for great anguish and grieving. Why do you think this is?

Sikhs believe that after death the soul appears before God and then its future is decided. In most cases, a person's soul returns to live another life in a new body. Or it may be that the soul is ready to remain with God, its development being at last complete.

Guru Arjan had in mind union with God when he said, 'Meet the Lord of the universe. Now is the time to meet him: after a long time you have been given human form.'

The decision as to whether a soul is ready to remain with God lies always in the hands of God. A decision cannot be forced on God by pointing out all of the rituals one kept or prayers that one said. A life of great goodness may help, but no one can gain release from reincarnation as a matter of right. Release comes only with God's acceptance. God graciously may decide one's soul is ready and so union with God is granted. Union with God depends ultimately on the grace of God.

2 Why do you think Sikhs are cremated rather than buried when they die?

3 In groups of three or four, plan a 5–10-minute documentary on 'Reincarnation'. Your documentary may include:
- a survey of views
- an interview
- a short piece of video.

4 'The claim that when we die we have to answer for how we have lived is only told in the hope that people will behave better.'

Write a few sentences explaining whether you agree or disagree with this statement. Give a reason to support your view.

Sikh prayer

objective

to consider what Sikhs believe about prayer

glossary

Gurmukh
Guru Nanak
Manmukh
Waheguru

Sikhs pray wherever and whenever they want and for however long they like. As with other religions, there are prayers which are recited from the holy book, both in private or in a gurdwara each morning or evening. There are different prayers for different times of the day and for different occasions.

Many Sikhs also meditate either by sitting quietly and thinking of God, repeating the name of God, **Waheguru**, or by listening to Sikh hymns. Any of these methods allow a Sikh to spend some time where their whole mind is focused on God.

A Sikhs praying together in a gurdwara.

> One day, when Guru Nanak was talking to some holy men they invited him to go to their place of worship. In the place of worship, every time the leader prayed Guru Nanak smiled and began to laugh. Not surprisingly everybody in the building was annoyed.
>
> 'Why are you laughing?' the Guru was asked.
>
> But Guru Nanak wasn't being mischievous or making fun of their leader. He realised that when the leader prayed, his heart and mind were not really on God. The leader admitted that this was true and that his prayers were not genuine.

> 1 What are the similarities and differences in the ways Sikhs and members of *one* other religion that you have studied communicate with God?

Is prayer enough?

There is a famous story about **Guru Nanak**, the first great Guru of Sikhism.

B Sikhs praying privately at home.

Sikhism teaches that prayer isn't always a good thing. Guru Nanak taught that prayer can become a barrier to communicating with God if it just becomes a mindless, repetitive ritual. Sikhs do not believe that just praying to God will guarantee that God will favour a person. Prayer doesn't make any difference if the prayer is just mechanically repeating words.

Sikhs also believe that praying to God does not guarantee that a person will be rewarded after they die. Just as Guru Nanak seemed to be able to see into the hearts and minds of people and recognise fake prayer, so too can God recognise fake prayer or prayer that is not properly motivated.

However, Sikhs do believe that prayer can help a person achieve union with God. Simple, direct and honest prayer is a part of daily life for most Sikhs. Such prayer can help a person overcome faults like greed, anger, selfishness and pride. It can help a person to become more 'God-minded'. Sikhs call this **Gurmukh**. Without prayer in one's life, a person may become only interested in their own selfish desires or worldly pleasures. Sikhs describe such people as being 'worldly-minded' or, to give them their proper name, **Manmukh**.

However, prayer alone is not enough. It is our actions, our good deeds, which will also decide whether a person can break free from reincarnation.

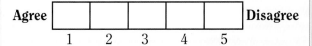

2 a 'If a person prays to God often, then God will be more likely to help that person in any life to come.'

   Using the scale 1–5 below, decide whether you agree or disagree with the statement above.

   Agree | | | | | Disagree
   1   2   3   4   5

   b Discuss your response with a partner or in groups of three. Suggest some good reasons to support your view.

3 'A person who has lived an honest life full of good deeds will always be accepted by God, even if they have never prayed or even believed in God.'

   Write a paragraph explaining why you agree or disagree with the statement above.

Sikhism and art

Art is important in Sikhism as a way of expressing and deepening religious faith. Sikhs have found ways of making the faith accessible and popular to millions of ordinary people through art. This can be seen in Sikh architecture, in visual images, in poetry and, for some, most importantly of all, in music.

objective

to examine the role of the arts in Sikhism

glossary

Guru
Guru Granth Sahib
Kirtan
Takht

The reader

Canopy

Takht

The Guru Granth Sahib

Gholak (collection box)

Pathway to the living Guru

A Inside a gurdwara.

1 a Imagine standing in the place shown in photo **A**. Write up to 10 words describing how you would respond or feel in that place.

   b First, snowball your ideas in pairs, then in groups of four, and finally as a class. Divide the class into three groups. Each group agrees on at least *five* words to best describe the feelings of most people in that group. Post up your words for the other two groups to see. Does this place arouse similar feelings or responses in most people? Explain why these feelings are aroused in these places?

Activity

Sikh interior design

Photo **A** shows the main prayer room inside a gurdwara (a Sikh place of worship) in Britain. The interior design of many prayer rooms is very similar. The floor is usually covered in white sheets of cloth. This gives the room a sense of cleanliness and purity. There is often a number of coloured sheets that seem to form a pathway. The pathway leads to the part of the prayer room on which the eye naturally focuses, which is the **takht**. The takht is like a covered throne. The takht is where the Sikh holy scripture, the **Guru Granth Sahib**, is kept.

Gurdwara prayer rooms tend to be large, open spaces. Although there might be symbols or pictures of the **Gurus** on the walls, often prayer rooms are quite plain. People often say that in such a space they have a feeling of uncluttered stillness. In many prayer rooms there is then a sense of cleanliness, purity and stillness and also a sense of tranquillity, peace and serenity.

2 Prayer rooms in gurdwaras and other places of worship are usually designed to create the right type of atmosphere for worship. Design your own prayer room. If you are not religious, then design a room where you can relax and be peaceful.

3 When you have designed your room, write a short explanation for why you have chosen the colours, layout and objects that you have.

Sikh painting

Another important form of Sikh art is in the form of painting. Sikh artists have painted famous events in the lives of the Gurus. These events often show qualities that are highly prized in Sikhism, for example courage, humility and compassion.

However, when it comes to painting, the most frequently seen form of Sikh art is portrait painting. Often this takes the form of painting portraits of the Ten Gurus.

Many of these portraits show the Gurus in a similar pose, dressed in the same way and looking very much alike. This is probably deliberate. It is thought by some to represent the Sikh belief that all of the Ten Gurus were enlightened by the same teaching and that they all taught the same one message.

Some Sikhs feel that it would be better if there were no paintings of any of the Gurus. They believe that a portrait of a Guru encourages idol worship. However, there is no real evidence that this is happening in Sikhism.

Sikh music

Music in Sikhism is seen as being a sacred art. The early traditions of Sikhism make it clear that Guru Nanak embraced music. He saw it as a valuable way of teaching others. As he travelled through different villages and towns, Guru Nanak would sing his own songs. His close friend, Mardana, would accompany the Guru using a stringed instrument, called a rebeck. Often what they played was based on popular folk tunes. This was the early beginnings of **kirtan**, the singing of praise to God.

Today, the singing of kirtan in Sikh worship is as popular as ever. It is seen as a joyful way of expressing one's love of God. Kirtan is also valued as a bond which unites all people. It isn't something only trained priests do in their temples. It is a way of bringing all people together, the old and the young, men and women, those who cannot read and those who are highly educated.

4 Plenty of top-selling songs written in recent years are about faith or have a serious moral message. For example, Pink 'Family Portrait' and Black Eyed Peas 'Where is the Love?'

Choose a song you like which you think has something important to say. Explain what you think the song's message is and why you like it.

15

The influence of the Gurus

Is there anybody who has influenced your life? Is there somebody about whom you think, 'I wish I could be like them'? If there is, it might be said that that person has authority in your life.

> **1** Who do you think provides a good role model for young people today? Think about this quietly on your own. When you have a name, share your answer with a partner giving your reason. As a pair, share your answers with another pair. Report back your answers and your reasons to the rest of the class.

In Sikhism there are ten people who all Sikhs deeply respect and admire. These ten people are known as the Ten Gurus. A Guru is above all a teacher. The word 'Guru' is an ancient Sanskrit word which means 'teacher'. When it comes to what Sikhs believe and how a Sikh should behave, all of these Ten Gurus have authority.

Sikhs do not believe that any of the Gurus are God. The Gurus are not gods, they are not the sons of God and they are not angels.

All of the Gurus are human beings so they are never worshipped. However, they are deeply loved and even revered.

A Guru may be a teacher of the sort who stands or sits in front of others and talks. All of the Ten Gurus taught in this way.

However, the Gurus also taught by setting an example. In the way in which they lived their life, and through their character, the Gurus provided a vivid example of what it means to live life as a true Sikh.

A Guru may also teach in a way that seems strange. A Guru may do something which suddenly jolts a person into seeing the truth. By doing so, a Guru can be a channel to God.

An example of how a Guru may teach in a way that seems strange can be found in the story of *The Emperor and the Guru's kitchen* on the next page.

The Emperor and the Guru's kitchen

A One day, Emperor Akbar decided to visit the leader of the Sikhs, **Guru Amar Das**. When Emperor Akbar arrived at the Guru's village he was surprised. Instead of special treatment being made at his arrival, the Emperor was simply given a message from the Guru. It said, 'First eat together then meet together.'

Emperor Akbar and his wealthy attendants were puzzled. They could see no grand banquet for them. Instead, the people in the village pointed to the Guru's kitchen. In the Guru's kitchen all the people in the village sat on the ground and ate together. No fine wines or rich delicacies were served. The food was clean, simple, and always free.

Akbar's attendants looked disgusted. But Akbar thought for a moment or two, and then he smiled. Akbar walked into the Guru's kitchen and sat down. Reluctantly, Akbar's wealthy friends joined him. In the Guru's kitchen Akbar was given the same food and was treated like everybody else.

After he had eaten, Akbar met the Guru. As they greeted, Emperor Akbar bowed and said, 'Thank you Master. Today I have learnt a valuable lesson.' The Guru looked deep into the Emperor's eyes and smiled.

Sikhs believe that all of God's teaching could not be expressed in a single lifetime. So, as each Guru came to the end of their life, they nominated their successor, a new Guru. Through that new Guru, God continued to speak. The name and the body of each of the Ten Gurus were different but the same spirit of the Guru lived in all.

This continued until the tenth Guru, **Guru Gobind Singh**. When Guru Gobind Singh felt that his death was very close, he realised that the line of human Gurus had come to an end. From now on the holy book, the Guru Granth Sahib, was installed as a Guru. Authority was no longer to be found in a human Guru.

The spirit of the Guru was now in the holy book. However, the spirit of the Guru was also to be found in the Sikh community itself. Sikhs do not believe that one single person alone has the authority to decide on all matters to do with religion or life. Instead, Sikhs believe in the authority of what the Sikh community decides when they are together in the presence of the Guru Granth Sahib.

2 Read story A. What do you think the Emperor learnt on the day he visited Guru Amar Das?

Activity

3 What are the advantages and disadvantages of a faith which has one leader or head who has the final decision on all matters to do with religion and belief?

4 'The spirit of the Gurus lives on in the Guru Granth Sahib and the Sikh community.'

How would you explain this statement to a Year 6 pupil?

Activity

B All gurdwaras today contain a langar, or 'Guru's kitchen', where everyone is welcome and everyone sits and eats together.

The living Guru

objective

to consider what Sikhs believe about the authority of the written word

glossary

Gurmurkhi
Punjabi
Vak lao

Listening to God's words

There is a famous story involving Guru Nanak and his close friend Mardana.

> One day, after many hours of travelling, Guru Nanak and Mardana stopped to rest. Mardana was busy tying up a horse when the Guru spoke. 'Mardana, touch the chords, the Word is descending.'
> 'But master,' Mardana replied, 'If I let go, the horse may run away.'
> Guru Nanak looked at his friend, there was a gentle calmness in his voice, 'Let the horse go, Mardana.'

At particular moments in his life Guru Nanak was aware of inspired words coming to him. Some people might think that these words came from Guru Nanak's own imagination. Guru Nanak himself believed that these words came to him from something outside of himself.

When Guru Nanak says, 'the Word is descending' he is expressing his belief that the particular words he is thinking of at that moment are different from other words which come from his own mind. He believed that, at particular moments in his life, what he was about to say or sing was coming down to him from God.

This is why the holy book of Sikhism, the Guru Granth Sahib, has such authority in the lives of millions of Sikhs. The Guru Granth Sahib has authority not because it happens to be written by great poets or wise people. It has authority because the book is thought to be the result of extraordinary moments in the lives of some people. At those moments, these people felt inspiration was coming to them from God.

The words which Guru Nanak felt were inspiration coming to him from God formed the beginning of the Sikh holy book. But the Guru Granth Sahib does not contain only the words of Guru Nanak. The book also contains what are believed to be the inspired words of the second, the third, the fourth, the fifth and also the ninth Guru.

Sikhs believe that the Guru Granth Sahib is the holy book which provides the basis for their views about God and life. However, Sikhs recognise and respect that God-inspired writings can be found in other holy books.

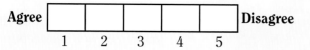

1 a 'There is no such thing as inspired writing that comes from God. If a person writes something which is wise, it comes from them as a human not from God.'

Using the scale 1–5 below, decide whether you agree or disagree with the statement above.

Agree | | | | | Disagree
1 2 3 4 5

   b Discuss your response with a partner or in groups of three. Suggest some good reasons to support your view. In a large circle, share your view with the rest of the class. Participants may choose to speak, listen, or listen initially and speak later.

Asking the Guru…

In the early years it was the Ten Gurus who provided Sikhs with advice and guidance on matters of daily life and belief. For over 200 years, from the time of Guru Nanak until the death in 1708 of Guru Gobind Singh, the tenth Guru, it was the words of the Gurus that largely governed the actions of Sikhs. However, shortly before he died, Guru Gobind Singh declared that the holy book was to be the Guru. The Guru as a living person was replaced with a holy book, the Guru Granth Sahib. In fact, the Guru Granth Sahib is thought of as a living Guru. The Guru Granth Sahib is written in the **Gurmurkhi** script. It is read in **Punjabi**.

Activity

2 a Look at picture **A** below. What shows you that the Guru Granth Sahib is being treated with respect, and as a living Guru?

b Discuss with a partner what this may suggest about Sikh beliefs today, or how Sikh beliefs have changed over time. Report back your ideas to the rest of the class.

A The Guru Granth Sahib being read in a gurdwara.

This practice of asking the Guru still exists today. However, no longer is a human Guru asked to decide. Instead, the custom is of asking the holy book. Many Sikhs do this daily. The Guru Granth Sahib is opened at random and a verse from the book is read. The verse that appears is thought by many Sikhs to have advice which will help them through the day. This is called **vak lao**. Vak lao means 'taking God's word'.

Activity

3 a Sikhs believe their holy book, which was written hundreds of years ago, can still provide helpful guidance for solving the problems of the twenty-first century.

Choose a passage, or perhaps a teaching, from a holy book you know which you think provides helpful guidance. Explain what passage you have chosen and why you think it is helpful.

b Are there any problems that you don't think a holy book could help with?

What is the truth?

objective

to consider what Sikhs believe about religious truth

glossary

Khanda

How do you know whether or not something is true? The main source of truth in science comes from accurate and careful observation. In science, for something to be thought of as true the idea would have to be rigorously tested. Experiments would have to be made and those experiments would be repeated by other scientists in order to check that an error had not been made.

With religion, on the other hand, the main source of religious truth comes from God as revelation. Listed below are five beliefs which most Sikhs would agree to be true:

1 There is one God.
2 God is the creator of all things.
3 All living things have a soul.
4 The soul cannot die.
5 All of the Ten Gurus were inspired by God.

These beliefs are not based on the scientific method of using accurate and careful testing. They are believed to be 'religious truths' revealed by God.

1 Are there things that you believe to be true, but which cannot be proven in any scientific sense of the word? If so, why do you believe them to be true?

All religions claim that their beliefs and teachings are true. However, such claims to religious truth raise some very difficult questions. For example:

● How do we know if a religion is true?
● Is it possible to prove that a religion is true?
● Is there evidence that a religion is true?
● Is there only one true religion?
● Can all religions be true?
● Can a religion be partly true?

Sikhs do not believe that all religious beliefs are true. Guru Nanak even sometimes gently made fun of people if he thought that their religious beliefs were wrong.

Sikhs do not believe that religious truth is only to be found in Sikhism. Ever since the early days of the Gurus, Sikhs have always shown a great deal of respect for other religions. Many Sikhs would accept that it makes little difference whether you use a prayer mat, pray in a particular building or fast on a certain day. These are seen as rather shallow differences between religions.

A We are one!

Some call themselves Hindus

Others call themselves Muslims

Among these are Shi'ah and also Sunnis

Yet man is one race in all the world.

God as Creator and God as Good

God in his Bounty and God in his Mercy

Is all one God. Even in our errors

We should not separate God from God!

Worship the one God.

(Poem written by Guru Gobind Singh)

Poem **A** is saying that it does not matter which religion you follow. What is really important, many Sikhs believe, is that a person should be trying to follow God's path, the way of true religion. Following the true religion has more than anything else to do with compassion, faith, goodness of character and commitment, rather than which particular faith a person belongs to.

Sikhism, and the other great religions, if honestly undertaken, may help a person to follow God's path. Behind the different truths each religion teaches, there lays an eternal truth, the oneness of God.

B People from different faiths worshipping together. The symbol on the boy's turban is of a **khanda** – a two edged sword.

Activity

2 Compare the Sikh belief that religious truth can be found in other religions with another faith that you have studied.

3 Write a letter to appear in the letters page of a local newspaper expressing your view on the claim: 'All religions are more or less the same.'

Sikhism and science

Religion and science have sometimes clashed over what is true and what isn't true.

A Galileo was put on trial in 1633 because he claimed that the earth wasn't at the centre of the solar system, but that the sun was.

While these arguments were happening particularly in Europe, there were no similar arguments between scientists and Sikhs. In the Guru Granth Sahib, and in the teachings of the Ten Gurus, there are no claims about the movement of the sun or the planets. Nor in Sikhism are there to be found detailed claims about God's creation of life on earth.

The words of the Sikh holy book and of the Ten Gurus are really about spiritual, moral and religious matters. The passage in the Guru Granth Sahib that comes closest to telling the story of how the universe began describes things before creation, not creation itself.

Because of this, Sikhs do not have any difficulty with scientific ideas or theories. Sikhs, in general, welcome new scientific theories and new technological developments. This includes the theory of evolution, the Big Bang theory, the internet, mobile phones and interactive whiteboards.

'For millions of years there was nothing but darkness over the void. There was neither earth nor sky, only the Infinite Will. There was neither night nor day, sun nor moon and the Lord was in a state of trance.'

(AG 1035)

1 Explain why Sikh beliefs do not conflict with scientific theories about the creation of the universe.

Sikh scientists

In fact, many Sikhs have welcomed science and some have become trained scientists. Many Sikhs use their skills and scientific knowledge as doctors, nurses, farmers, teachers, and as businessmen and women to help improve the lives of thousands of people.

For example, Dr Harinder Singh Bedi is a renowned Sikh heart surgeon. His skill at open heart surgery has saved the lives of many people.

Another example of a Sikh scientist who has helped others through his knowledge is Dr Gurdev Singh Khush. Dr Khush is one of the world's experts on the science of plants. He has improved rice plants so that, instead of being able to grow only one tonne of rice on their land, farmers are able to grow five or even as much as eight tonnes of rice. As the world's population has grown, the work of Dr Khush has prevented the likely starvation of millions.

B Dr Harinder Singh Bedi.

C Dr Gurdev Singh Khush.

Science vs. religion?

Although it is true that there have been no arguments between Sikhism and science, is it really true that Sikhs are not at odds with science? J.B.S. Haldane, a famous British scientist of the twentieth century, claimed that religion and science will always be in conflict.

> There can be no truce between science and religion.
> (J.B.S. Haldane b.1892)

J.B.S. Haldane believed that the main source of truth in science comes from accurate and careful observation. In science, for something to be thought of as true, the idea would have to be rigorously tested. Experiments would have to be made and those experiments would be repeated by other scientists in order to check that an error had not been made.

This perhaps partly explains why science and religion so frequently clash. Some scientists do not accept 'religious truths' to be 'truths' at all because they cannot be observed, cannot be tested and cannot be checked by others.

2 Choose *one* of the statements below and write a few sentences stating whether you agree or disagree. Explain why. You could ask other people what they think and include their thoughts in your answer.

- 'Science has done more good in the world than religion.'

- 'Science is dangerous and, unless checked, could destroy human life on this planet.'

Assessment for Unit 1

'The famous shrine the Ka'bah, the House of God, is in the city of Makkah. While on his travels Guru Nanak visited Makkah. When it became dark the Guru went to sleep in the cool open air. Early the following morning a man angrily woke him up. Guru Nanak sleepily said, "My good friend, what is the matter?" "Your feet," the man shouted, "You are sleeping with your feet towards the House of God. Your feet are pointing at God."

"Do not be angry my friend. Please, turn my feet in the direction where God cannot be found." The man bent down and picked up the Guru's feet. But then the man was puzzled. "The direction where God cannot be found… where was that?" Gently the man put down Guru Nanak's feet. The man looked at the Guru and bowed his head and left the Guru's feet where they were.'

(Janam Sakhi *Travels of Guru Nanak*)

These questions test different sets of skills in RE. Which skills do you need to work on? Choose the level you need and work through the tasks set.

Level 3

- In what way did the angry man's understanding of God change throughout the story?
- Sikhs believe that God is everywhere. What other words would they use to describe God? What beliefs about God do Sikhs claim are not true?
- Sikhs claim that having a belief in God helps them through life. How do you think having a belief in God can help a person through life? What beliefs are important to you that help you with life?

Level 4

- Describe *three* sources of authority a Sikh could turn to if they wanted to know what was right or wrong.
- Choose *one* other religion and try to think of *three* sources of authority a follower of that faith could turn to.
- How do you decide what is right or wrong? Are there any sources of authority that are important to you? Explain which you value most, and why.

Level 5

- Describe what Sikhs believe happens after death.
- How do their ideas differ from your own views of life after death? Are there similarities between your beliefs and Sikh beliefs?
- Think of a question you would like to ask a Sikh about life after death. How do you think they might answer?

Level 6

When interviewed, the Oxford University Professor Richard Dawkins was asked the following question:

Interviewer: 'Now a lot of people find great comfort from religion. Not everybody is as you are… well-favoured, wealthy, has a good job, happy family life… not everybody's life is good and religion brings them comfort.'

Dawkins: 'There are all sorts of things that would be comforting. I expect an injection of morphine would be comforting… it might be more comforting, for all I know. But to say that something is comforting is not to say that it's true.'

- Is the fact that God brings comfort a convincing argument for the belief in God?
- Suggest *two* arguments why a person might say God does exist.
- Suggest *two* arguments why a person might say God does not exist.

Who is responsible?

From a Sikh point of view, simply being alive is a fantastic privilege. All around us there are things of amazing beauty and of endless fascination. Extraordinary though it is, life on planet earth is not perfect. There are many inequalities, there is conflict and anger, and there are people who experience great misery, loneliness and rejection.

For Sikhs and non-Sikhs, these inequalities and injustices raise many questions.

- How do Sikhs decide what is right or wrong?

- What are Sikhs' views about family life and living as a citizen?

- What are your views? Who is responsible?

Living as a saint soldier

objective

to consider Sikh views about the Five Ks and the concept of being a saint soldier, and how this affects the lives of young Sikhs in Britain today

glossary

Amrit
Five Kakke / Five Ks
Guru
Guru Gobind Singh
Kacchera
Kangha
Kara
Kesh
Khalsa
Kirpan
Panj Piare
Rehat Maryada
Sant-sipahi
Sikh

Sometimes doing what you know is right might mean hardship and sacrifice; it might mean showing moral courage. It might mean being jeered at by others or falling out with friends. Sometimes doing what is right means a person has to be like a soldier and take a stand.

Guru Gobind Singh, the tenth **Guru**, knew all about being like a soldier and taking a stand for what you believed in. He had seen his own father put to death while taking a stand protecting the right of people to believe in their religion.

Throughout the period when Guru Gobind Singh was Guru, and for over the next hundred years, life for all **Sikhs** was very difficult. Frequently, Sikhs were imprisoned, tortured and cruelly put to death.

To deal with such brutal intolerance, Guru Gobind Singh taught his followers to be like soldiers and take a stand for what they believed in. Guru Gobind Singh, however, taught Sikhs to be not like ordinary soldiers. Instead, every Sikh was to be like a saint soldier or a **sant-sipahi**. A saint soldier battled in their day-to-day life for what is good, fair, right and just.

The Sikh uniform

To reinforce this idea that a Sikh was to be like a saint soldier, Guru Gobind Singh encouraged all Sikhs, like soldiers, to wear a uniform. The uniform consisted of five symbols. These five symbols are known as the **Five Ks** or the **Five Kakke**. Wearing the Five Ks has come to symbolise a Sikh saint soldier who takes a stand for what they believe in, and is prepared to live life according to what is good and just.

Activity

1 Research *one* of the Five Ks. Find out about its origins and what it symbolises for Sikhs today.

2 What are the benefits and drawbacks a Sikh may experience wearing the Five Ks that you have researched?

Kacchera – shorts.

Wearing the Five Ks is seen by most Sikhs as being an essential part of the Sikh way of life. In 1945, many leading Sikhs, after much discussion, agreed on a Sikh code of life. This code of life was called the **Rehat Maryada**. The Rehat Maryada said that a true Sikh 'must believe in the necessity and importance of **Amrit**'. Amrit is a special initiation ceremony. To take Amrit, a believer must be of an appropriate age to make that decision. Amrit is a commitment to wearing the Five Ks but it is also a commitment to the Sikh code of life. By taking Amrit, you join the **Khalsa**. The **Panj Piare** were the first members of the Khalsa.

A Each of the Five Ks is often given its own symbolic meaning.

Kesh – uncut hair.

Kangha – a comb.

Kara – a steel band.

Kirpan – a sword.

I chose to take Amrit because to me the Five Ks are a symbol of who I am, where I come from and what I believe in.

(Arrandeep Singh, aged 14)

Activity

3 In photo **B**, Arrandeep speaks of his decision to take Amrit and commit himself to the Sikh way of life. Think about something that you have decided to make a commitment to, such as supporting a football team or joining a club. Write a few lines explaining why you chose to make that commitment and the impact this has had on your life.

4 'To be a true Sikh a person doesn't have to wear a turban, or leave their hair uncut. A person can be a true Sikh on the inside.'

What does the above statement mean?

What's right and wrong?

objective

to look at the way Sikhs decide what is right and wrong

glossary

Gurmukh
Guru Granth Sahib
Guru Nanak
Manmukh

How do you decide what is right and wrong? Decisions about what is right and wrong are called moral decisions. Life is full of moral decisions.

1 Draw a mind map or spider diagram showing all the things that help you make decisions about what is right and wrong.

The Sikh code of conduct

How does a Sikh decide what is right or wrong? To help with moral decisions, most Sikhs will be guided by the teachings of the Ten Gurus and the words of the **Guru Granth Sahib**. Some moral decisions are very clear and there is little disagreement amongst Sikhs as to what is right or wrong.

In the Rehat Maryada (see page 26), the guide to the Sikh code of life, there are laid down some very clear rules.
For example:

- Sikhs should not take alcohol, drugs such as opium, or other intoxicants, or use tobacco.
- No Sikh should gamble.
- No Sikh should steal.
- Sikhs must not commit adultery.
- A Sikh's daughter should marry a Sikh.

While most Sikhs would agree with these rules, not all Sikhs do. Some Sikhs, for example, do drink alcohol and believe that this does not conflict with their religion or with the teaching of the Gurus.

Ever since the days of **Guru Nanak**, there developed within Sikhism some important moral principles. If Sikhs are uncertain about what is right and wrong, often these moral principles can help believers to find an answer. On the next page are four of these important Sikh moral principles.

Be a saint soldier
Like a saintly soldier showing discipline and self-sacrifice, train yourself to develop virtues like courage, self-control, patience and humility.

 A Four Sikh moral principles.

Be God-centred
Do not strive for worldly, materialistic goals like wealth, fame, lust or what is fashionable. Do not be self-centred (**manmukh**) but be God-centred (**gurmukh**).

Treat people equally
Do not distinguish between people on the basis of colour, caste, religion, sex or social status.

Be a householder
Do not cut yourself off from the world like a hermit. Live like a lotus, rooted in the muddy pond that is the world, but do not let yourself be corrupted by the world.

The story of the Sikh water carrier has been very influential for Sikhs. This influence continues today (see pages 48–49 on Khalsa Aid).

The story of the Sikh water carrier

Many Sikhs were being tortured and put to death by the Emperor's army. Led by their tenth Guru, Guru Gobind Singh, the Sikhs were forced to defend themselves. A battle takes place between the Emperor's army and the Sikhs, led by Guru Gobind Singh.

When the daylight faded the fighting stopped. The Emperor's army went back to their camp and the Sikhs returned to their fortress knowing they would have to fight again the next day to survive.

In the evening light a Sikh water carrier called Ghanaya could be seen on the battlefield. Many on the battlefield were dead but Ghanaya found some of the Sikh soldiers were alive. He gave the wounded Sikh soldiers water and what help he could.

But then Ghanaya heard a voice, 'Please, do you have some water for me?' The voice was of a badly wounded soldier but he wasn't a Sikh. He was one of the Emperor's soldiers. Ghanaya then noticed there were other men. They also badly needed water and they also were soldiers of the Emperor.

B

Ghanaya's problem

What should Ghanaya do? Should Ghanaya give water only to the wounded Sikh soldiers? Or should he give water to the wounded Sikh soldiers and also to the wounded Emperor's soldiers?

2 a With a partner, discuss Ghanaya's problem in story **B**. What should he do? Try and make use of a Sikh moral principle to answer Ghanaya's problem.

   b Share your answer with *two* other people, and then with the whole class.

3 a Find out how *The story of the Sikh water carrier* ends. See www.nelsonthornes.com/religionsandbeliefs.

   b Did Ghanaya apply a Sikh moral principle correctly? Explain your answer.

Sikh family life

objective

to find out what
Sikhism teaches
about family life

glossary

Guru Har Gobind
Guru Har Krishan

Sikhism teaches that choosing to share one's life with another by
becoming a husband or a wife requires a great amount of commitment.
To have children and to bring them up so that they become decent
human beings requires patience, love, understanding and personal
sacrifice.

At the time of the Ten Gurus, many people believed that a truly holy
person would live life as a 'sannyasin'. A sannyasin was a person who left
their family to live alone like a monk or a recluse. By doing so, they
believed they could give themselves full time to prayer and meditation.
In this way, they believed they would find union with God.

The Ten Gurus rejected the idea of a sannyasin. Instead, they taught that
it was as a 'householder' or a 'grihastha' that union with God could be
achieved. A householder got married, had children and earned money to
pay for food and other needs. A person could be truly holy while living
life fully as a family man or woman. While some religions suggest that
the noblest way to live life is as a monk or a nun, Sikhism teaches that
the noblest way to live life is by living with others as part of a family.

A Sikh family in
the UK today.

B Holy person.

As an example to their followers, all of the Gurus married and had children, with the exception of **Guru Har Krishan** who died at the age of only seven. The Gurus were questioned as to whether it was really right for a religious person to be married. For example, on one occasion, a holy man called Shah Daulat asked **Guru Har Gobind**, 'How can you be a religious man when you do wordly acts, have a wife and children and possess worldly wealth?' The Guru replied, 'A wife is a man's conscience, his children continue his memory and his wealth gives him and his family sustenance.'

As well as the belief in family life, Sikhs also believe that they must earn a living. No one should expect to live off others or rely on charity to survive. Because of this, most Sikhs believe that it is important that they get a job and work hard and honestly.

This belief in work has brought a great deal of success to many Sikh families. Many Sikhs have worked hard to get a good education. This has resulted in Sikh families often having family members who are well qualified as teachers, engineers, builders, accountants, solicitors and ICT experts. Having such qualified people often benefits the family and makes the family stronger.

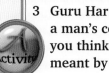

1 Look at photos **A** and **B**. Write a list of the differences in the lives of these people. What responsibilities does each person have?

2 Householder or hermit?

With a partner, arrange the six triangles below into a pyramid. Place the statement you agree with the most at the top. Place the two statements you quite agree with in the second row. Place the three statements you least agree with at the base of the pyramid. Explain the reasons for your arrangement.

A hermit who lives alone has the best chance of knowing God.

God doesn't object to wealth if it has been earned honestly and one is willing to share.

The noblest way to live life is by not marrying and devoting one's life to God.

In a family, people become bad tempered and unhappy.

Wealth and possessions get in the way of serving God.

3 Guru Har Gobind said, 'A wife is a man's conscience...' What do you think Guru Har Gobind meant by these words?

The noblest way to live life is by living with others as part of a family.

Family dilemma

Respect for the older members of a family is widespread all across India and throughout Asia. Many Sikh families in Britain believe that if there is a problem in the family, then the advice of an older member of the family should be sought.

The older member of the family may be the father or mother, but it may be an older uncle or aunt, or a grandfather or grandmother. An older member of a family is often seen as the head of a family. Their views often have great influence. It is believed that their age and experience of life have given them wisdom.

Age can bring wisdom. However, not everyone shares this view.

(A)

It is time that Balvinder got married.

(Balvinder's parents.)

Balvinder's dilemma
Balvinder is a very able 21-year-old Sikh girl. She has completed a law degree. Balvinder hopes to go on and become a solicitor. Her father, Simran, has received numerous offers for Balvinder's hand in marriage. Simran has selected a young man whom he considers to be suitable. He shows Balvinder a photo of this young man and asks her if she would meet him. At the meeting Balvinder will have a chance to see and talk to Ramjeet.

Activity

1 What should Balvinder do? Should she obey her father and go to the meeting, or should she try to persuade her father that she should continue her studies and train as a solicitor and that marriage can wait? In groups of three or four, discuss Balvinder's dilemma.

The meeting of the two families goes ahead. Following the meeting, Balvinder tells her parents that she can't stand Ramjeet. She says he is old fashioned and is a 'male snob who doesn't respect the views of women'. Her parents like Ramjeet and are disappointed that their daughter does not like him. They tell Balvinder that when she gets to know Ramjeet better, she will like him. Simran tells his daughter that Ramjeet is a 'proper Sikh' as he is an **Amritdhari**. This means that he is a Khalsa member who wears the Five Ks.

> One day, I hope to be a solicitor.
> (Balvinder.)

B

2 What should Balvinder do now? Should she obey her father and go to the second meeting, or should she tell her father to cancel the meeting as she will never marry Ramjeet? Discuss Balvinder's dilemma in your group.

Activity

> You wouldn't have to worry about such matters...
> (Ramjeet.)

C

Balvinder tells her parents that there is a young man called Ajaib whom she likes. Ajaib left the college a year ago and is now at university studying to become a doctor. Balvinder has never spoken to Ajaib but she thinks that he shares many of 'her views'. Ajaib is not an Amritdhari Sikh and he has his hair cut short. He is a **Sahajdhari** Sikh. Balvinder says to her parents, 'If I have to marry, can you arrange a meeting with Ajaib's family and our own and, if it works out, then I will marry Ajaib?'

> What a person wears doesn't matter. I am a Sikh on the inside.
> (Ajaib.)

D

3 What should Balvinder's parents do? Should they stand by their original wishes that their daughter should marry Ramjeet, an Amritdhari Sikh, or should they organise a meeting with Ajaib's family, even though this may result in their daughter marrying a Sahajdhari Sikh?

Activity

The Sangat

A community

Sikhs have a strong sense of belonging to a community. In that community they share many common values and beliefs. Sikhs, in the main, do not feel that they are alone in this world with only themselves to rely on. They feel that they are part of a faith community. They call that faith community the **Sangat.**

Sikhs believe the Sangat should meet together often. This is why Sikh places of worship, **gurdwaras**, are often full of people.

A Sikhs worshipping in a gurdwara in the UK.

Guru Nanak taught that much unhappiness and misery is caused because people feel that they are on their own. Although they might have the freedom to be an individual, for many this can easily lead to depression. Guru Nanak taught that being part of a faith community brought great benefits. The Sangat, he believed, should be a getting together of good people. If a Sikh regularly meets up with good people, it brings about a change in that person. By being in the Sangat a person can learn what goodness means and learn from the good example of others. In a faith community people become less selfish. They learn how to get on with others. They can share their problems and get help. They can talk about the beliefs which give their life meaning. Also in the Sangat, people learn to care about others.

objective

to consider Sikh beliefs about the Sikh community

glossary

Gurdwara
Langar
Sangat
Vand ka channa

1 In groups of three or four, choose *one* of the following statements to discuss. Do you agree or disagree with your chosen statement? Report back your ideas to the rest of the class.

- 'You cannot be deeply religious on your own; you have to practise your faith with others.'

- 'The lack of a sense of community has brought many problems like mental illness, depression and selfishness.'

- 'Being part of a faith community limits a person's freedom to think for themselves.'

B Sikhs serving food in a langar.

One reason why Sikhs have a strong sense that they are members of a faith community is because of the **langar**. The langar is a free kitchen. Every gurdwara has a langar. The langar is a large space where everybody in the gurdwara can sit down and enjoy a meal together. All food served in the langar is free. It doesn't matter whether a Sikh is rich or poor, young or old, male or female, from a distinguished family or a humble family. All members of the Sikh Sangat are welcomed into the langar and there they will all eat together.

In the langar it is strictly forbidden to have a special table for so-called 'important people'. No one is allowed to sit on a special chair or have a special cushion to raise them up and make them look more important than anyone else. In the Sikh Sangat everyone is an equal member.

Even non-Sikhs are welcomed into the langar. Christians, Buddhists, Jews, Hindus and Muslims all are welcomed. Whether a person is religious or has no religious faith at all, every visitor to a gurdwara will be invited into the langar and will be offered a free meal. The langar has not only developed the Sikh sense of being a member of a community, it has also been an important way of giving help to the needy. For hundreds of years any person who was desperate could visit a gurdwara where they would be offered food. Sikhs do not begrudge this. In fact, Sikhs regard it as an honour to serve a traveller, a pilgrim or simply a visitor to their gurdwara.

How can Sikhs afford to be so generous? The answer is that Sikhs do not try to help the poor by acting just as individuals on their own. Instead, Sikhs work together like a team. Sikhs believe in community effort or **vand ka channa** – 'divide and share'. Each Sikh puts in what money, food or work they can to support the langar. With everyone making an effort it adds up, making it possible for the faith community to be very generous.

2 You have been asked to interview a member of the local Sikh community for a local radio station. The subject is, 'Living in a faith community'. Prepare a list of questions you intend to ask.

3 Guru Nanak once defined a truly religious person in the following way:

'Religion does not consist in words, but a religious person is one who looks on all persons as equal.'

Working with a partner and using no more than 30 words, suggest your own definition of a truly religious person.

Men vs. women?

All of the Sikh Gurus spoke up for the rights of women. In an age when men dominated society, Guru Nanak said that women should be respected: 'It is through woman, the despised one, that we are conceived and from her that we are born… Why denounce her, the one from whom even kings are born?'

The Gurus taught that it is wrong to despise women or treat them as inferior to men. All humanity, women as well as men, were to be treated equally. The honour of reading the holy scripture is not seen as one for which only men are worthy. Women also are given the honour of reading the Guru Granth Sahib.

(A) The honour of reading the holy scripture or leading prayers is not seen as one for which only men are worthy.

There are many stories of women who played an important part in the development of Sikhism. For example, women like Bebe Nanaki, Mata Khivi, Mata Gujri and Mai Bhago are deeply respected in Sikhism.

Bebe Nanaki was Guru Nanak's elder sister. She supported Guru Nanak's work. She persuaded Mardana to accompany Guru Nanak on his missionary tours. It was Bebe Nanaki who bought Mardana a rebeck. Mardana played the rebeck while Guru Nanak sang his hymns. This played a part in establishing the tradition of using hymns and music as a part of Sikh worship.

1 In groups of three or four, brainstorm examples of women being treated unfairly or not enjoying the same rights as men. Write your examples on Post-It notes and put them on a display board for the rest of the class to see.

2 Can you think of any examples of religions treating men and women differently? Two possible examples of this might be:

   ● women not being allowed to become bishops

   ● women being required to worship in a separate area of a place of worship.

Another woman who was important in the early development of Sikhism was Mata Khivi. Mata Khivi was the wife of the second Guru, **Guru Angad**. Mata Khivi played a major part in establishing the tradition of the langar. She worked day after day to make sure hundreds of people were fed. Although she came from a wealthy background, often she did menial work like serving out the food herself. When they first saw this many people were shocked. Why would an aristocratic, wealthy lady serve food herself? Surely that was a job for servants? However, it also provided a clear example of what the Gurus were teaching, that all people should be treated equally and that menial work wasn't to be sneered at.

Although in Sikhism the belief is that women and men are to be treated equally, this is not always what appears to happen. Some claim that boys are given more freedom than girls.

Nihal and the birthday party

Nihal is a 12-year-old Sikh girl. She is popular, very chatty and has strong views. One of her friends at school, Sara, invites Nihal to her birthday party at her house next Saturday. Sara will be 13 years old. Sara's mother and father will be at the party and there will also be quite a few girls and boys.

Nihal asks her mother and father if she can go to the party. Her father says no. Nihal says he is being unfair as her 15-year-old brother, Satbir, has been to parties and he went to his first party when he was 12 years old. Nihal's father says Satbir is different. If she went to a party, people would talk about her. The honour of the family, he says, depends on everyone in the family being respectable.

What do you think Nihal should do?
Should she:
● respect her father's decision and not go to the party, accepting that he probably knows best
● put up with her father's decision, but sulk making it clear that she is not happy
● sneak out of the house next Saturday and go to the party
● undertake a protest, refusing to eat at family meals, speak to her father or be helpful around the house
● go to the party, but agree that her father will go with her?

3 a What do you think Nihal should do?

   b Explain what you think the consequences might be, and how you think the story might end. Take into account Sikh beliefs in your answer.

Sikh citizens

Guru Nanak didn't want his followers to be just private citizens who put up with injustices going on around them. Nor did Guru Nanak believe that a Sikh should passively accept everything leaders, governors, kings or emperors did. If an emperor was in the wrong, Guru Nanak was prepared to tell them so. 'Speaking truth to power' is an important aspect of Sikh teaching.

On one famous occasion in 1520, Guru Nanak witnessed the savage invasion of the military leader Babar. Babar pillaged many towns and cities and forced thousands into captivity. Guru Nanak himself was taken prisoner. Recognising his special qualities, Guru Nanak was taken to Babar. Instead of being intimidated by the War Lord's presence, Guru Nanak insisted that Babar should release all of his prisoners. He told Babar that his duty was to 'be just to all'. Babar was deeply moved by the Guru's words and from that moment onwards he respected the Sikhs and made a real effort to be a just ruler.

Maharaja Ranjit Singh

For many Sikhs the best example of Sikh citizenship can be seen in the rule of the great Maharaja of the nineteenth century, Maharaja Ranjit Singh. Ranjit Singh ruled a large area of north east India from 1801 until his death in 1839, a period of almost 40 years. His deep belief in Sikhism was a major influence on how he ruled and how he believed all of the citizens he was responsible for should behave.

1 a How do you think Guru Nanak managed to persuade Babar to change his mind?

b Imagine if Guru Nanak had met any of today's world leaders, what do you think would have happened?

A Maharaja Ranjit Singh the Sikh ruler of the Punjab for almost 40 years.

Ranjit Singh established a state based on Sikh beliefs. Everyone worked together, regardless of their race, religion or social background. All people were encouraged to view each other not as people separated by religion or class competing against each other, but as people sharing and working together as fellow citizens.

Ranjit Singh actively encouraged tolerance and respect for all religious traditions and also for those who held no religious beliefs. He promoted people not on the basis of their religion but on the quality of their character and their ability. One of his closest advisors, Aziz ud Din, was a Muslim. His finance minister, Dina Nath, was a Hindu. He encouraged fairness, generosity, learning and respect for life. He abolished capital punishment. His army were issued with permanent orders that, 'no religious place, no religious book, no place of learning, no standing crop was to be destroyed and no woman dishonoured'. He banned tax laws which discriminated against people on the grounds of their religion.

During his reign, Ranjt Singh established such a sense of peace and mutual respect amongst his people that many flocked to live as citizens in his empire.

Activity

2 Choose *one* of the statements below. State whether you agree or disagree with your chosen statement. Explain your answer.

- 'If we ignore injustice and don't act against it, then injustice will win.'

- 'Religion has no business getting mixed up with politics.'

3 In what way did Sikh principles and beliefs influence Ranjit Singh's way of ruling? Give examples and justify your answer.

4 Find out what is meant by a 'secular society'. Is a 'secular society' the same as an 'anti-religious society'? Explain your answer.

Parm Sandhu is a Chief Inspector for the Metropolitan Police and is one of the most senior female Asian police officers in the UK. She is an example of a British Sikh working as a good citizen contributing to British society. She was the winner of the 2006 Public Sector Asian Women of Achievement award which is for women whose primary focus is on the contribution that they can make to society through the work that they do. What else can you find out about her?

B What does it mean to be a good Sikh citizen today?

39

Speaking out

When Guru Nanak told the War Lord Babar that his actions were wrong, he did so using words which were very clear. Telling a man who is known to have murdered and enslaved thousands that he has been cruel and unjust is, of course, a very dangerous thing to do. Babar could easily have been angered by the Guru's words. The War Lord might well have ordered his guards to take the Guru outside and cut his head off.

A Guru Tegh Bahadur was beheaded for telling Emperor Aurangzeb that he was wrong.

'Speaking truth to power' involves running great risks. It involves immense courage. Following the example set by Guru Nanak's, there have been many Sikhs who have bravely spoken up telling powerful and dangerous leaders the truth when they were in the wrong.

Guru Tegh Bahadur told Emperor Aurangzeb he was in the wrong as he was trying to smother the right of people to practise their religion (in this case, Hinduism). Because he spoke up, Guru Tegh Bahadur was forced to watch three of his close friends being tortured to death. Finally, the Guru himself was beheaded.

> 'Hinduism may not be my faith, and I may believe not in the supremacy of Veda or the Brahmins, nor in idol worship or caste or pilgrimages and other rituals, but I would fight for the right of all Hindus to live with honour and practise their faith according to their own rites.'
>
> (Guru Tegh Bahadur)

1 Can you think of any other people who have been killed for their beliefs?

Devindar's dilemma

Devindar has an older brother called Harjit. Harjit is 17 years old. Devindar overhears Harjit boasting that he and three of his friends chased a 'black kid' into a park. She hears Harjit saying, 'I punched him and we all kicked him several times as he ran away. He had it coming as he pushed past us and called us, "Paki".'

That following morning Devindar reads in a local newspaper that a young black male has been admitted into hospital with a broken jaw following an attack from a gang of Asian youths. The report says he was chased into a park and kicked several times. Police suspect the attack was racially motivated.

Activity

2   In groups of three or four, discuss Devindar's dilemma. What should Devindar do? In your discussion bear in mind the Sikh teaching that sometimes it is necessary to show moral courage and be prepared to 'speak truth to power'.

3   'Speaking truth to power' may involve showing moral courage by speaking up even though it might be dangerous. In groups of three or four, prepare and act out a short play during which a person does or says something that shows moral courage.

4   Maharaja Ranjit Singh was a Sikh leader who ruled a large area of northern India from 1801 until his death in 1839. With a partner, find out what you can about the way Ranjit Singh governed. In what way did Sikh teaching influence him as a governor?

B Devindar and Harjit.

Assessment for Unit 2

'Whoever calls himself a teacher but who lives on the charity of others, never bow before him. He who earns his livelihood by the sweat of his brow and shares it with others, knoweth Nanak, only he can know the way.'

(Guru Nanak, Guru Granth Sahib page 1245)

These questions test different sets of skills in RE. Which skills do you need to work on? Choose the level you need and work through the tasks set.

Level 3

- Look at the photo of the person begging on a street in Britain and read Guru Nanak's saying. Write *three* things Guru Nanak says about how a person should live life properly.
- What reasons might be given for walking past a person begging on a street in Britain? Are these reasons convincing?
- What do you think a person should do if they see a young man begging on a street in Britain? Explain your answer.

Level 4

- Give *two* examples of ways in which Sikh Gurus have shown people how to behave.
- Explain why it is important for Sikhs to live life as a saint soldier (sant-sipahi). Describe the impact the idea of being a saint soldier may have on a Sikh's life.
- Describe an occasion when you did something for someone else and got nothing out of it. What made you do it? Were you right to do what you did?

Level 5

- Explain why some Sikhs believe they should take responsibility for the welfare of people whom they have never met.
- Explain the connection between the practice of running a langar and Sikh beliefs.
- Why do you think Sikhs get involved in challenging authorities that abuse human rights? Do you think the rights of humans who live in distant countries should be of less concern to us compared to the rights of humans who live nearby? Explain your answer.

Level 6

- Explain why some Sikhs feel it is their duty to speak out against injustice. If a person who speaks out against injustice ends up getting murdered, may they still have achieved something worthwhile? Explain your answer.
- Compare the way a Sikh makes decisions about right and wrong actions with the way a non-religious person decides. What sorts of things guide your decisions about right and wrong actions?
- Why might Sikhs find fulfilling some of their religious duties difficult in today's world? Should religions remain unchanged, or are there acceptable ways in which religions can change as the world changes? Explain your answer.

We're not on our own!

Poverty, conflict and the environment are some of the biggest issues facing humans today.

- What do Sikhs have to say about world poverty? How do they respond to it as an issue?

- Do Sikhs have ways of tackling poverty from which we can learn?

- What does Sikhism have to say about the environment and about war and conflict?

- Are there examples of Sikhs in the world who have confronted these issues? What have they done and how can we learn from their examples?

Sewa

Every year over nine million people die from hunger. This means that every hour over a thousand people die due to hunger.

The **Sikh** view is that such poverty is simply wrong. All human beings, Sikhism teaches, are part of the same human race. Sikhs believe that we are all created by the same one God. Because we are all in a sense brothers and sisters, it is wrong to be indifferent to the suffering of fellow humans, wherever they are in the world.

Sikhism teaches that any person who shrugs their shoulders and does not care is flawed in their moral and spiritual development. They are far from showing the qualities a person must have if they are to achieve the great goal in life – union with God. For Sikhs, then, every person should be joining in the battle against poverty. By doing so, they will be helping to reduce the suffering their fellow human beings have to endure.

However, Sikhs have a second reason for caring. A person who cares deeply about the needs of others shows the qualities which God favours. Because of this, they may be specially favoured by God and be close to escaping rebirth. It is possible that they are near the end of a long spiritual journey. They may be close to finding union with God.

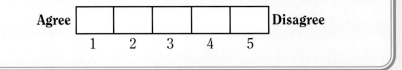

1 Choose *one* of the following statements. Using the scale 1–5 below, decide whether you agree or disagree with your chosen statement. Explain the reasons for your answer.

- 'Only people who believe in God have a strong reason for doing something about poverty in countries far away.'

- 'People who don't believe in God are actively tackling world poverty just as much as people who do believe in God.'

Agree | | | | | Disagree
     1   2   3   4   5

All of the Sikh **Gurus** showed the deepest concern for the poor. They encouraged their followers to reach out and help the poor. For example, one day the third Guru, **Guru Amar Das**, noticed a young boy called Jatha who made a living selling boiled grain. Often the boy would freely give away grain to the hungry and to poor labourers. Impressed by Jatha's generous spirit, the Guru blessed the boy. Eventually, he appointed Jatha as the fourth Guru, **Guru Ram Das**.

objective

to consider what Sikhism teaches about poverty

glossary

Gurdwara
Guru
Guru Amar Das
Guru Nanak
Guru Ram Das
Langar
Sewa
Sikh

Global issues: poverty

44

Actions speak louder than words

Kindness and generosity towards others are important virtues in Sikhism. However, Sikhism also teaches that it is not right for a person who is poor to sit around blaming others or to feel sorry for themselves. Sikhism teaches that virtues like self-help, hard work and showing initiative are important when it comes to overcoming poverty.

A This man is helping to build a gurdwara for no money, as an act of sewa.

One story about **Guru Nanak** tells of how, when visiting a village, the Guru was shocked to see people living in dirty slums. Guru Nanak set fire to the slums. He then helped the villagers to build clean, new homes to replace those destroyed.

This practice of willingly doing things for other people is, for many Sikhs, simply a natural thing to do. It is what many Sikhs have been taught from an early age. It is called **sewa**. Sewa means 'giving service to others'. Sewa may involve cleaning dishes in the **gurdwara**, cleaning the floor or handing out food in the **langar**.

However, sewa isn't just something you do for other Sikhs in the gurdwara or in the Sikh community. Sewa also means 'giving service' to the wider community, to humanity in general. Sewa is always given without any thought of reward or personal benefit. Sewa is, however, seen as essential if a Sikh is to make spiritual progress. By undertaking sewa, a Sikh gains the highest merit in the eyes of God.

Activity

2 Arrange the six triangles in **B** into a pyramid to show which statements you agree with the most. Place the statement you agree with the most at the top. Place the two statements you quite agree with in the second row. Place the three statements you least agree with at the base. Explain the reasons for your arrangement.

By teaching young people to show kindness and generosity.

We can't, so don't worry about it.

How do we put an end to extreme poverty in the world?

Start by getting rid of corrupt governments in poor countries.

By making rich countries pay a lot more for products like chocolate, coffee and bananas.

B

By making use of GM crops and building irrigation projects.

Tax rich people more heavily like footballers and celebrities.

Putting teachings into practice

One of the practical ways in which Sikhs are expected to do something about poverty is by giving. A Sikh is expected to work hard and honestly to be able to support themselves and their family. However, any extra money left over should not just be fritted away on the latest luxury electrical product, fashion item or expensive leisure pursuit.

1 Copy and complete the table below listing luxury electrical products, non-essential fashion items and expensive leisure pursuits.

Luxury electrical products	Non-essential fashion items	Expensive leisure pursuits

In Sikhism, the tradition has been that a Sikh should give at least a tenth of their earnings to others. This practice is called **dasvandh**. Dasvandh may be given in the form of money or it may be a donation of food. If a new gurdwara is being built, a Sikh may even give dasvandh in the form of building materials like bricks, wood or sand.

When Sikhs give dasvandh, they believe that it is important to give without a sense of pride, or a feeling that they are being noble. This is because Sikhism teaches that any income a person has comes from God. Giving away a tenth of your income is therefore not seen as a generous sacrifice, it is seen as returning to God, the Giver, what rightly belongs to God.

I think a religion having a set amount for giving is a very good idea because then you cannot feel guilty about whether that was enough to give or not.

(Katie.)

2 Is Katie (shown in photo **A**) right? Draw a mind map or a spider diagram showing the advantages and disadvantages of a religion having a set amount for giving.

Activity

Birmingham to London Charity Bike Ride

As well as giving, many Sikhs are regularly involved in fundraising for good causes. For example, every year the Sikh Arts and Cultural Association, based in Southall, organises the Birmingham to London Charity Bike Ride.

The ride starts in Birmingham. For two days, about 250 riders pedal the 140 miles or so, eventually to be greeted by cheering crowds when they arrive in London. Large numbers of Sikhs take part in the ride. However, people of other faiths, or of no religious faith, also support the event.

The Sikh community organises a place for the cyclists to stay overnight. Most of the marshals and assistants are also Sikhs. They offer help and give water and refreshments to the riders. Over the years, the event has raised thousands of pounds for good causes including: The Red Cross; Cash for Kids; Contact a Family; and Ealing Hospital.

B The Annual Birmingham to London Charity Bike Ride.

3 Find out more about the Birmingham to London Charity Bike Ride. Write to: The Sikh Arts and Cultural Association, PO box 90, Southall, Middlesex UB2 4RU.

4 Imagine you have been asked to interview a Sikh rider on The Birmingham to London Charity Bike Ride for a local radio station. With a partner, prepare up to eight questions for the interview. Rehearse the interview with your partner, anticipating how your questions will be answered. Focus mainly on *why* questions rather than *when, where* or *what* questions.

5 a Find out about any local or national projects in the UK that help the poor and hungry which Sikhs may be involved in. For example:
  - The Bradford Curry Project.
  - The Rebridge Sewa Bike Ride.
  - Sikh Union Coventry Charity Walks.

b Write and design an advert for a magazine for *one* of these projects.

Khalsa Aid

Fundraising and giving money to charities are important ways in which Sikhs can do something to help people who are poor. However, Sikhism also teaches that helping others with your own hard work and labour is also very important.

objective

to consider an example of Sikhs responding to poverty and need

glossary

Khalsa

In the past, the Gurus very rarely just handed out money and told others to get on with the work. More often than not they led by example, clearing the ground, carrying the bricks and helping with the digging themselves.

Of course, giving to a charity is better than not giving anything at all. But putting money into a collection tin and then not thinking or caring any more about the problems of others is not enough. Sikhism teaches that giving money should not become a substitute for action. It must not become a cheap way of buying an easy conscience.

A Ravinder Singh, founder and chief co-ordinator of Khalsa Aid.

A role model

There are many examples of Sikhs who are at work today trying to relieve the suffering caused by poverty. One such person is that of a British Sikh living in Slough. His name is Ravinder Singh.

In 1999, military forces mounted a campaign of murder and persecution in the province of Kosovo. Thousands of Kosovans, in fear of their lives, crossed over the borders into neighbouring countries. With many penniless Kosovans struggling to survive in makeshift camps, Ravinder Singh and just a few friends got together to talk. They asked themselves what could they do to help? And so **Khalsa** Aid was born.

Ravinder Singh and his friends contacted Sikh gurdwaras in Southall and Slough. Members of the Sikh community gave generously but the plan was not to simply send money to a charity to do the work. The plan was for Sikhs themselves to roll up their sleeves and, with their own hands, bring help to the people of Kosovo.

Within two weeks of the appeal going out, Khalsa Aid had organised two trucks and a van packed with food, blankets and other aid materials. In convoy, Sikh drivers drove the three vehicles through Belgium, Germany and on into Eastern Europe. In a town called Lac in Albania the convoy arrived and was able to provide much needed food to over 3,500 refugees. The convoy drove on into more dangerous territory. Again, they were able to provide food and additional aid to two other Kosovo refugee camps.

B Khalsa Aid in action.

This was to be the first of many successful aid missions organised and carried out by volunteers working for Khalsa Aid. Later, in the same year, Khalsa Aid helped the victims of a cyclone in Orissa in India. In 2001, working with local Sikhs, Khalsa Aid workers helped distribute clean drinking water and put up tents for the victims of the Gujarat earthquake in India.

Ravinder Singh and other Khalsa Aid volunteers have repeatedly shown enormous levels of courage. They have often spent weeks away from the easy and safe life they could enjoy in Britain to help people living in highly-dangerous parts of the world like Rwanda, Somalia and Afghanistan.

1 Research and report back to the class examples of dangers Khalsa Aid volunteers have had to face. See www.nelsonthornes.com/religionsandbeliefs.

Khalsa Aid's work still goes on. Its volunteers helped in the clean up operations following the 2004 Boxing Day Asian tsunami. Khalsa Aid volunteers also travelled to Kashmir to help people who were made homeless because of a massive earthquake in 2005.

In all of its work, Khalsa Aid and Ravinder Singh, its founder and chief co-ordinator, have kept to the original plan. They do not just send money to relief organisations and charities to do the work. British Sikhs volunteer to work for Khalsa Aid. They travel to parts of the world in need of help. They assess first hand what needs to be done and, working with local people, they do the work themselves.

2 Arrange a class debate on the following idea: 'Before starting work every young person should spend several months abroad doing voluntary work.'

3 'We don't hear enough about the good things religions do, we only hear about the bad.'

Write a few lines explaining whether you agree or disagree with this statement above. You may wish to use the example of Khalsa Aid, or another religious charity that you have studied, in your answer.

God's world

objective

to consider what
Sikhism teaches
about the
environment

glossary

Guru Arjan
Guru Granth Sahib

A Tree logging.

1 Draw a mind map or a spider
diagram to show the questions
photo **A** raises for you.

The environment is thought by some to be the most
important issue for the twenty-first century. Regularly,
concerns are raised about forests being cut down.
Questions are asked about the ozone layer. Anxiety is
expressed about pollution in our air and water. Fears are
raised about global warming.

2 'People who leave lights and TVs on, who always drive rather than
walk, who turn up the central heating rather than put on a jumper,
are helping to destroy the planet for humans in the future.'

a With a partner, carry out a survey amongst friends and family.
Do they agree or disagree with the above statement? You may
wish to ask those you survey to rate their response using a scale
of 1–5 (1 = totally agree, 5 = totally disagree). Ask those you
survey to explain their answer.

b Analyse your findings and report back to the rest of the class.

Given this bleak picture of the future, Sikhs, of course, are very concerned about the environment. But what does Sikhism teach about the environment?

In the stories and sayings of the Ten Gurus it is clear that they had a lot to say about things like justice, honesty, family, the dignity of labour, service to others, sharing, and respect for women. But in the sayings of the Gurus, and in the words of the **Guru Granth Sahib**, the environment, the ozone layer, deforestation and global warming are not mentioned.

This should come as no surprise. When the Gurus were teaching, the impact humans may be having on the environment was not an issue anyone was talking about. It was not until long after the Gurus had died that the environment was seen as a problem.

There are stories which show the Gurus were worried about fresh water. Guru Amar Das, for example, built a water well at Goindwal. **Guru Arjan** also built a large water system in the village of Chheharata. The system provided fresh drinking water. It also irrigated the land so that crops could be grown and the area was green generally.

Sikhism clearly teaches that God is the creator of the universe. Sikhism also teaches that God watches over the universe.

'The Creator Himself created the Creation. He produced the Universe, and He Himself watches over it.'

(The Guru Granth Sahib page 37)

Sikhism also teaches that creation is a manifestation of God. That is, in creation, God may, in a sense, be found.

'The Creator created Himself and created all Creation in which He is manifest. You Yourself the bumble-bee, flower, fruit and the tree.'

(The Guru Granth Sahib page 466)

From passages like the ones below in the Guru Granth Sahib many Sikhs believe that they have a responsibility to God to care for the planet. The earth, in fact the whole universe, belongs to God, as God created it. God is also closely connected to the earth and all life upon it. The earth is sacred. Robbing the planet of life or polluting its atmosphere is therefore wrong.

3 Read the statements in **B**. Which statements do you agree with? Which *two* statements do you think Sikhs would agree with the most?

Humans in the future will curse us because we didn't take the environment seriously.

Don't worry about the environment, as new technologies will solve the problem.

We have a special responsibility to God to care for the planet.

B

Individuals can't save the planet, as industry and business are the problems.

We must abandon extravagant lifestyles and live simpler, more spiritual lives.

We can carry on with our lives because what happens in the future isn't our problem.

Caring for God's world

Sikhism teaches that we have a special responsibility to God to care for the planet. The earth and the whole universe are sacred as God created them. All life is in unity and in all life God is manifested.

When it comes to looking after the environment what do Sikhs do to put these ideas into practice? For many Sikhs, one important way in which they try to limit damage to the environment is by starting with themselves and their own lives. For many Sikhs, this means not living a life driven by consumerism.

Sikh's believe that they should strive for spiritual progress. The wish to have more and more consumer goods gets in the way of making spiritual progress. Guru Nanak made this clear in the words shown opposite:

Sikhs remain active in the world. They do not renounce the world for a life of dull poverty. But they reject a showy and mindless materialistic life. Many Sikhs live a fairly simple life and so the harm they do to the environment is kept to a minimum.

'Then why get attached to what you will leave behind … all your houses, horses, elephants … they are just pomp and show. All totally false.'

(Guru Nanak)

1 'Many Sikhs live a fairly simple life.' List examples of the ways in which a Sikh may live a 'fairly simple life'.

2 Choose *one* of the following statements. Do you agree or disagree with your chosen statement? Explain why.

   Activity

   ● 'Living a "fairly simple life" means living a life which is boring, flat and dull.'

   ● 'Even though we know about the damage we're doing to our planet, we're still not thinking about what we buy.'

Another way in which Sikhs have responded to worries about the environment is by installing solar panels in gurdwaras. In India, there are some 28,000 gurdwaras. All of these gurdwaras run a langar – a free kitchen. This means the Sikh community provides free food to thousands of people a day. The five largest gurdwaras in Delhi alone feed more than 10,000 people every day. Cooking food for such a large number uses up a lot of fossil fuel. Of course, even more fossil fuel would be needed if all of these people prepared their own food at home.

Sikh leaders tackled the problem by installing solar panels in eight of Delhi's largest gurdwaras. Solar panels provide a much more environmentally-friendly source of power. Gurdwaras in the villages and countryside are also being fitted with more fuel-efficient cooking equipment. This will help bring down energy use by 15%.

Some large purpose-built gurdwaras have surrounding land. In many cases, the Sikh community makes a special effort to cultivate this land, providing parks and gardens for everyone in the local community to enjoy.

Growing trees and plants in such areas makes a valuable contribution to the environment. Trees act as sponges. They soak up toxic carbon dioxide (CO_2) in the air. The carbon is stored in the tree. The tree then releases oxygen (O_2) into the air, which we need to breathe.

A Solar panels have been installed in the biggest gurdwaras in Anantapur.

B Gardens around a gurdwara.

3 All large buildings like gurdwaras, churches, schools, factories and offices use up valuable energy. With a partner, visit *one* local place of worship and try to find out how well they are saving energy. You might draw up a list of questions or things to find out. For example:

- Do they use low-energy bulbs?

- Are unnecessary lights switched off and saver switches used on photocopiers?

- Is there a box for recycled paper?

- Are urns and kettles overfilled?

- Is cycling or walking encouraged?

- Could solar panels or wind turbines be installed?

Activity

Sikh environmental projects

In their daily lives, many Sikhs make sure that they are doing 'their bit' for the environment. They may do this by buying a modest car that has a low fuel consumption rate. They may ask for goods at the supermarket checkout not to be put into new plastic carrier bags but, instead, reuse old bags. They may collect rainwater for use in their garden and so avoid using fresh drinking water.

Although these might seem small, all of these measures add up and do make a difference.

However, some members of the Sikh community have come up with much more active environmental schemes. For example, Baba Sewa Singh is a Sikh living in northern India. Baba Sewa Singh was not interested in telling the government that it had to do something, nor did he want to run a campaign telling other people not to waste energy. His plan was not just to cut down on how much air pollution he was responsible for but to do something positive that would make the air cleaner.

In 1999, Baba Sewa Singh launched his own massive tree planting project. He persuaded 21 volunteers to help him. Putting into practice the Sikh principles of hard work and the dignity of labour, day after day the team dug holes and planted saplings.

The trees were planted along all the roads which lead to the city of Khadoor Sahib. Working at a rate of over 14 trees a day, by 2004, Baba Sewa Singh's team had planted over 27,000 trees.

Inspired by Baba Sewa's work, 44 farmers in the region also began planting trees. Today, over 250 acres of land in the area is made up of orchards that provide local people with valuable fruit. Baba Sewa Singh has turned the area surrounding Khadoor Sahib into a green belt of lush vegetation.

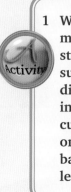

1 Write a letter to the manager of a local DIY store or supermarket suggesting that the store displays the sign shown in picture B to encourage customers to cut down on the use of plastic bags. Try to make your letter persuasive.

Today, Baba Sewa Singh and his team continue to plant trees. In order to establish a pollution-free environment, particularly around places of worship, Baba Sewa Singh has planted trees in the grounds of gurdwaras in Markana and in Gwalior. More volunteers have joined the project. With advice from the Punjab Horticulture Department, all of the trees are looked after and maintained.

It is not just in the Punjab in India that Sikhs have been involved in environmental projects. In 1999, Harbant Kaur Sehra worked for Nottingham Council as a community development worker. 1999 marked the 300 year anniversary of the foundation of the Khalsa. In order to celebrate the event, Harbant's idea was to organise the planting of Khalsa Wood. Khalsa Wood was to consist of 300 trees. One tree for each year of the Khalsa. The wood was to be established in an uncultivated piece of land in Bestwood Country Park in Nottingham.

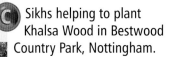
Sikhs helping to plant Khalsa Wood in Bestwood Country Park, Nottingham.

On the morning of the planting, despite pouring rain, 600 members of the Sikh community showed up. All helping each other and often working under umbrellas, the small army got to work. By the end of the day, 300 oak saplings had been planted. A further 200 saplings were planted the following year. And over the years, some 500 more trees have been added.

Khalsa Wood, although created by the Sikh community in Nottingham, brings benefits to everyone. Khalsa Wood helps reduce CO_2 in our atmosphere. But the wood is also a place of recreation and leisure. Every day it is open to all members of the public.

2 a Which *one* of the following views do you agree with the most? Explain your answer.

- 'Getting stuck in and physically doing the work yourself inspires others to feel that they should be doing something and so they join you.'

- 'Doing the work yourself just encourages people to be lazy and to avoid taking responsibility themselves.'

b Which *one* of these views do you think most strongly represents Sikh teaching? Explain your answer.

3 When talking about the creation of Khalsa Wood, Harbant Kaur said, 'If we do something in the name of religion, like voluntary work or giving to charity, we are very keen.'

Do you agree with Harbant Kaur's remark? Do you think religion is a strong motivator, encouraging people to do good voluntary work?

4 Do you think people are taking the issue of the environment seriously enough? Explain your answer.

Sikh teachings about conflict

objective

to find out what Sikhism teaches about conflict

glossary

Guru Gobind Singh
Kirpan

War, or a conflict of any kind, is a dreadful thing. In any conflict there is always suffering. No matter how sophisticated the weapons, no matter how carefully a battle may be planned, there are always casualties. There are always innocent people who suffer.

Sikhism teaches that war is never a good thing. War is always evil. None of the Sikh Gurus approved of war. However, they did teach that war sometimes is a necessary evil that is right to undertake.

When a tyrannical leader abuses the rights of others and tries to take over, when talking fails to work, when innocent people are being imprisoned or murdered, then, and only then, Sikhism teaches that war is the right action to take. Sikhism doesn't teach that war is a good thing, but it does teach that, as the very last resort, war is sometimes sadly necessary.

In a famous letter called 'The Zafarnama' written by **Guru Gobind Singh**, the tenth Guru, to Emperor Aurangzeb, Guru Gobind Singh rebukes Aurangzeb. He accuses him of breaking his peace treaties and of acting like a tyrant, murdering people for no reason.

Guru Gobind Singh called for peace. But the Guru warned Aurangzeb that, without peace, fighting is justified. Aurangzeb failed to respond and Guru Gobind Singh was true to his word. He rallied his followers and fought a fierce war in defence of the Sikh community.

A

'You occupy the throne in the name of the Lord but strange is your justice, shedding the blood of people without reason.'
'When all efforts to restore peace prove useless and no words avail, lawful is the flash of steel, it is right to draw the sword.'

'The Zafarnama' – letter to Emperor Aurangzeb from Guru Gobind Singh.

B Guru Gobind Singh led his troops into battle many times in defence of Sikhism.

1 a Working with a partner, arrange the six triangles below into a pyramid to show which statements you agree with the most. Place the statement you agree with the most at the top. Place the two statements you quite agree with in the second row. Place the three statements you least agree with at the base. Explain your answer.

   b Which of these views are similar to Sikh teachings about war?

War is always wrong. It is better to die or to be enslaved than go to war.

It is wrong to sit around while innocent people are dying.

War isn't glorious or good but, to sometimes defend what we believe in, it is justified.

If there was no religion, there would be fewer wars.

If a cruel leader abuses the rights of others and all talks fail, war is justified.

War makes the problem worse. It is better to negotiate and compromise rather than go to war.

Sikhism teaches that conflict is not something that should be rushed into. Hitting back simply because a community feels offended or because they feel hard done by is not right. Force is only permitted if a community is under attack and it needs to defend itself. Using force is also only permitted when all attempts at reconciliation have failed. Aggressive war, fought in an attempt to win land or power, is never justified in Sikhism.

Sikhism teaches that war is not only justified in self-defence, war to defend others from injustice is also justified. Sikhs are not anxious to fight. However, Sikhs do believe that it is wrong to ignore injustice that is being inflicted on people. If something can be done to prevent oppression, it is right to take action.

The wearing of the **kirpan**, or the sword, is often described as a reminder of this aspect of Sikh teaching. Sikhs wear the kirpan not because they are always looking for a fight. Rather, it is worn as a symbol to remind Sikhs that sometimes, if threatened, freedom and justice have to be defended.

C The kirpan is worn as a symbolic reminder that, if threatened, freedom and justice have to be defended.

2 a Find out more about the circumstances in which 'The Zafarnama' was written. See www.nelsonthornes.com/religionsandbeliefs.

   b Was Guru Gobind Singh justified in his criticisms of Emperor Aurangzeb?

   c Do you agree with his belief that war is justified as a last resort?

3 'As it is a symbol, it would be better if Sikhs carried a small kirpan no longer than 3cm, not a blade 10cm long or even longer.'

   Write a short article for a newspaper expressing your views on the statement above. Include the reasons why a Sikh wears a kirpan in your article.

What about conflict in everyday life?

Sikhism teaches that the use of force is permitted as a last resort against evil. This was certainly the view of Guru Gobind Singh, the tenth Guru, but was that the view of Guru Nanak, the first Guru?

Sometimes it is claimed that Guru Nanak believed in non-violence. Indeed, some people have suggested that Guru Nanak was a **pacifist**. A pacifist believes that violence in any circumstance is wrong. In fact, a pacifist would say that it is better to run the risk of being killed, rather than taking the life of another person.

Guru Nanak was certainly a man of great calmness who never resorted to violence himself.

This story in the right-hand column above gives us a good idea of what Guru Nanak was like. All of his life his message was one of brotherly love. Even when insulted or provoked, Guru Nanak never seems to have lost his temper.

Guru Nanak, and his two close friends, Mardana and Bala, had been travelling for a long time. They were exhausted and hungry having had almost nothing to eat or drink for many days.
At last they came to a village and Mardana went to ask for help. Mardana was polite and friendly but the villagers just mocked and jeered him. Finally, with their insults, they drove him away.
Mardana was furious. Guru Nanak, however, showed no anger or bitterness. He suggested that they walk on. A little while later Guru Nanak asked his two friends to join him in prayer. His prayer went as follows:
'Almighty God, give us the strength to remain calm in such situations. Help us to understand these poor people. They deserve our compassion rather than our hatred, for they do not have peace of mind or happiness in their lives.'

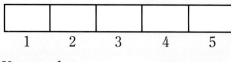

1 a Are you good at controlling your temper and avoiding conflict? On a scale of 1–5, rate your own behaviour.

1	2	3	4	5

Very good at controlling my temper and avoiding conflict.

Very poor at controlling my temper and avoiding conflict.

  b Anonymously record the number you rate yourself on a piece of paper. Collect all the pieces of paper for the class. Draw a bar chart to show the results.

  c Discuss the results:

   • Do members of the class generally think that they are good at staying calm?

   • Do many believe they are bad tempered and are poor at avoiding conflict?

2 Discuss the following questions with a partner or group, or spend some time thinking about them.

   • Is it important to avoid anger?

   • What things make you angry?

   • How do you think anger and conflict can be avoided?

Compassion, not hatred

Guru Nanak's belief seems to have been that if you were angry, this, in the long run, hurts you much more than anyone else. Anger damages your own spiritual progress and results in bad **karma**.

Bad karma would count against you in your next rebirth. Good karma would count in your favour and help you find union with God.

'Those who have the blessing of good karma, meet with the Lord.'

(Guru Nanak.)

Guru Nanak's peaceful and non-violent nature doesn't mean he was always opposed to war. When he met Babar, a man who had waged war in northern India, he didn't tell him all war was wrong. Instead, he told him that the taking of civilians as prisoners was wrong. Guru Nanak never had to deal with a tyrant who had murdered and imprisoned thousands of people and who refused to listen to reason. If he had, it is possible that he would have said that, as a last resort, fighting such a tyrant would be acceptable.

B Sikhs have a reputation for being friendly and helpful.

Taking the Gurus as their example, Sikhs in their day-to-day life often show a calm dignity. The reputation of most Sikhs is that they are friendly and helpful. As Guru Nanak encouraged, most Sikhs live by the rule that bitterness is best avoided and people who wrong us deserve our compassion rather than our hatred.

3 Make a list of what you think would give rise to bad karma.

4 Explain Sikh teachings about conflict in your own words. Make sure you include teachings about conflict in everyday life, not just teachings about war.

Activity

59

Conflict case studies

Violence

Sikhism teaches that war is sometimes justified. When Sikhs have fought they have often shown extraordinary courage and chivalry. Sikhs believe that if a war has to be fought, it must be fought with honour. Sikhism teaches that attacking civilians or humiliating prisoners is wrong. As a saint soldier (**sant-sipahi**), to fight in such a way would be thought of as a disgrace.

Sikhs have fought in the British army, and in the Indian army alongside the British, many times. Fearlessly, Sikhs have fought defending freedom and liberty. Often the British have had good reason to be grateful that Sikhs have been prepared to fight.

During the First and Second World Wars, many Sikh regiments fought alongside the British. Over 83,000 Sikhs died in the two World Wars. They fought in defence of their own lives and homes in India, but they also fought alongside the British and allied forces against fascism.

e Queen
eeting Sikh
ans who
ht in the
nd World War.

ssues:

1 a Read through the story of Naik Nand Singh in **B**. What discussion question does this story raise for you?

b First, share your question with a partner and agree on the best question. Then, repeat in groups of four. Share your group's chosen question with the whole class and vote to decide which *one* question the class should discuss.

c Form a large circle and discuss the class' chosen question which the story has raised.

The story of Naik Nand Singh

B

A famous Second World War engagement took place on 12 March 1943. A Sikh battalion was fighting against the invading Japanese army. The Sikh troops were pinned down by heavy machine-gun fire.

Sikh soldiers charged up the narrow track and attacked the first Japanese machine-gun position. Every one of the soldiers was killed or wounded. Their commander, Naik Nand Singh, although wounded, dragged himself to his feet. He ran on and, fighting alone, he captured three enemy gun positions. He was wounded six times in the action but killed over 30 enemy soldiers. For his actions in the face of enemy fire, he was awarded the Victoria Cross. This medal is the highest award that can be given for valour to a member of the British or Commonwealth armed forces.

Non-violence

Military force is not the only way in which Sikhs have responded to conflict situations. In the stories of the martyrdom of the fifth Guru, Guru Arjan, and the ninth Guru, **Guru Teg Bahadur**, we can see Sikhs using non-violence and self-sacrifice to confront evil. Non-violence has also been used by Sikhs to protest against unjust government.

Activity

2 Find out more about Sikhs' use of non-violence. See www.nelsonthornes.com/religionsandbeliefs.

3 'Non-violent protest is effective and also the noblest way to fight for any cause.'

Explain whether or not you agree with this statement. Use examples to support your case.

In 1923, in protest at the dethronement of the Maharaja of Nabha, the Sikh community organised a continuous reading of the Guru Granth Sahib, an Akhand Path. The reading was to take place in the Gangsar gurdwara in the Punjab. Large numbers of Sikhs gathered at the gurdwara. The local British authorities viewed such large numbers as provocative. People sitting in the gurdwara were arrested.

The Sikh community responded by organising squads of Sikhs to walk to the gurdwara to replace those who had been arrested. Every squad member took a pledge that said, 'My aim is to restart the Akhand Path. If, in doing so, I have to face hardship and trouble at the hands of the government officials, I shall bear all very politely and without lifting my hand to strike.'

The protest continued for over one year and 10 months until, eventually, all prisoners were released and Sikhs were permitted control of their gurdwaras.

The Hindu leader, Mohandas Gandhi, witnessed the non-violent methods used by the Sikh community. Later, Gandhi and Martin Luther King used very similar non-violent methods themselves.

C Today, there are still many Sikh regiments in the Indian armed forces. This battalion is part of the United Nations' peacekeeping force in Southern Lebanon.

Assessment for Unit 3

Level 5

These questions test different sets of skills in RE. Which skills do you need to work on? Choose the level you need and work through the tasks set.

Level 3

- The Guru Granth Sahib teaches that God is closely connected to the earth and all life upon it. Do you think we have a right to use animals for medical research? Give reasons to support your answer.
- Describe the circumstances under which Sikhs believe war may be the right action to take. Do you think war is ever the right action to take or is it always wrong? Explain your answer.
- Describe *three* ways in which Sikhs may offer help to the poor. What is your response to people collecting for charity outside a supermarket?

Level 4

- Describe *two* ways in which Sikhs have tried to reduce the harm they do to the environment. We all need to change the way in which we live to reduce environmental damage, do you agree or disagree?
- Sikhs believe that getting angry in the long run hurts those who get angry. Explain why Sikhs have this view.
- Many Sikhs believe that in affluent societies too much money is wasted on excessive consumption. Do you agree or disagree with this view? Explain your answer.

- Some Sikhs are vegetarians, while other Sikhs enjoy eating meat. 'What we eat is a private decision and has nothing to do with religion.' Do you agree or disagree with this statement? Explain why.
- Why might a Sikh refuse to fight? If a person is a citizen of a country, do they have a duty to fight if a war is declared? Explain your answer.
- Explain what inspires Sikhs to visit dangerous parts of the world in order to bring help to the needy. The 20 richest people in the world own more than the 48 poorest countries in the world. Do you think anything should be done about this? Why?

Level 6

- Many Sikhs say that there is nothing wrong with being very rich, as it means they can afford to be more generous helping the poor. Would you expect religious people to have a different attitude and give up everything they have to the poor? How might a wealthy Sikh respond to this view?
- Sikhism teaches that war is permitted as a last resort. Do you think Sikh beliefs would justify using nuclear weapons in a war if they were used as a last resort? How might a Sikh view the strengths and weaknesses of using nuclear weapons?
- What environmental challenges do you think Sikhs face if they accept they have a special responsibility to God to care for the planet? Do you think a non-believer has any responsibility towards the environment? Explain your answer.

Glossary

Amrit Liquid made of sugar and water that is used during ceremonies.

Amritdhari A baptised Sikh who keeps the Five Ks.

Atheist Someone who does not believe that God exists.

Code of life (See Rehat Maryada.)

Dasvandh 'Das' means 'ten', 'van' means 'share', together, they mean 'one tenth'. One tenth of a Sikh's earnings is used to support those in need, e.g. through a donation to the gurdwara.

Five Kakke or Five Ks The symbols worn by Sikhs.

Gurdwara Place of worship for Sikhs.

Gurmukh God-minded, living by the teachings of the Gurus.

Gurmurkhi The script that the Sikh holy book is written in.

Guru Teacher.

Guru Amar Das The third Guru (1479–1574).

Guru Angad The second Guru (1504–1552).

Guru Arjan The fifth Guru (1563–1606).

Guru Gobind Singh The tenth and final human Guru (1666–1708).

Guru Granth Sahib The holy book for Sikhs and the final Guru.

Guru Har Gobind The sixth Guru (1595–1644).

Guru Har Krishan The eighth Guru (1656–1664).

Guru Har Rai The seventh Guru (1630–1661).

Guru Nanak Founder of Sikhism. The first Guru (1469–1539).

Guru Ram Das The fourth Guru (1534–1581).

Guru Tegh Bahadur The ninth Guru (1621–1675).

Il Onkar A symbol that means there is only one God.

Kacchera One of the Five Ks – shorts worn as undergarments.

Kangha One of the Five Ks – a comb.

Kara One of the Five Ks – steel bangle or wristband.

Karma The teaching that what you do in this life influences what happens in the next life.

Kesh One of the Five Ks – uncut hair.

Khalsa The Sikh community.

Khanda Two-edged sword.

Kirpan One of the Five Ks – a sword or dagger, a symbol of peace.

Kirtan Singing of praise to God.

Langar The name for the dining hall and food served in a gurdwara.

Manmukh Worldly-minded, living by one's own selfish desires.

Mool Mantra First words of the Guru Granth Sahib, which sum up the most important beliefs of a Sikh.

Pacifist Someone who is against war and believes conflicts should be settled peacefully.

Panj Piare The group of five founded by Guru Gobind Singh.

Punjabi An Indian language spoken by most Sikhs.

Rehat Maryada Code of life for Sikhs. This lays down some rules by which Sikhs live.

Reincarnation The belief that when a person dies their soul is reborn into a new body.

Sahajdhari A Sikh who has not been baptised and who may keep some of the Five Ks.

Sangat A group of Sikhs who attend the same gurdwara. This group would make decisions together.

Sant-sipahi 'Saint soldier.' Guru Nanak taught Sikhs to be 'saint soldiers' or people who battle in their everyday lives for what is good, fair, right and just.

Sewa To serve humanity.

Sikh A pupil.

Takht Throne where the Guru Granth Sahib is kept.

Vak lao 'Taking God's word.' The name of the practice of opening the Guru Granth Sahib at random to provide advice and guidance for Sikhs today.

Vand ka channa The belief that Sikhs should pool their efforts and resources to provide more effective support to others. The words actually mean 'divide and share'.

Waheguru A popular chant that means 'Wonderful Lord'.

Index